With thanks!
Adm Oct 6, 2017

Also by Adam David Miller

Dices or Black Bones: Black Voices of the Seventies (editor)

Adam David Miller, A Sampler of His Poems (The Clamshell Press)

Neighborhood and Other Poems

Forever Afternoon

Apocalypse is My Garden

Land Between: New and Selected Poems

Ticket to Exile: memoir

Fresh Ink VI (co-editor)

The Sky is a Page

NEW & SELECTED POEMS

Adam David Miller

Eshu House Publishing
Berkeley, California

First Edition
Copyright © 2010, 2011 by Adam David Miller
All rights reserved.

Library of Congress Cataloging in Publication Data
Miller, Adam David
The Sky is a Page: New and Selected Poems
LCCN: 2009942140 (paperback)

Some of these poems have appeared in *TDR, Nimrod, Ba Shiru: A Journal of African Languages and Literature, The Black Scholar, Hypatia, Bottomfish, Synapse, Black Theatre, Paterson Literary Review, Good News, A Gathering of the Tribes,* and *The Addison Street Anthology: Berkeley's Poetry Walk.*

The art work incorporated into the cover design is "Bereshit," a pit-fired ceramic, by Susan Duhan Felix, 2008.

"Bereshit" is the first word in the Old Testament. It is translated as "In the beginning…" This piece was shown in Susan Duhan Felix's solo show at the Bade Museum in Berkeley, and is now owned by Adam David Miller. (www.susanduhanfelix.com)

Cover design and title pages by Jinny Pearce.
Photograph of cover art and author photo by Jinny Pearce.
Thanks to Linda Johnson, Swell Design, and Amy Wong, words & design.
Editorial assistance by Joyce Jenkins, with thanks to Richard Silberg.
Printing by McNaughton & Gunn.

Printed in the United States of America.

ISBN: 978-0-9656576-1-7

Orders, inquiries, and correspondence to:
Eshu House Publishing
P.O. Box 162, Berkeley, CA 94701-0162
(510) 845-8098
eshuhouse@gmail.com
www.adamdavidmillerpoet.com

CONTENTS

SUNSHINE WASH

CONJURES

Keep Sending Love Out

Keep sending love out
where the heart clutches and the soul sings.
Keep sending love out,
into the lighted dark, over the fog swept sea,
or where it runs the risk of dying dusty death.
Send it where there may not be an echo,
no return. Send love, that magic portent,
that drug of madness, the poet's bane, some fool's delight.
Send it where it has never been, a new address.
Keep sending, sending, sending

Walking Song

Limantour

From my back in the dunes,
Engorging the roar and the wash,
Eyes closed but for the shimmer world,
Half light on my lashes,
Winds cool the sun on my face.
With a single pant, a dog crashes by.

Sophocles and Matthew Arnold heard
This roar, and my uncle Benjamin?
No, only I,

the interminable cry of gulls soaring,
swerving, beating and calling, beating
against the wind or riding it.

The sea rolls out past Maui,
past New Caledonia, to Durban.
Winter solstice, closing down, storing up.

Sounds edge between boom
and wash.
Is there a sob under the roar?

It is a winter's beach, water bright sand.
Ocean, a lazy green, launches wave
upon wave, the retreating and returning sea.

The sky is a page to be written on.

Pt. Reyes Fault

Gulls working the wind,
eyeless Cheshire cat
fish-heads on the beach
as the two push upwind
against swirling sands.

—This bit of land here
was once 500 miles south.
—It was?
—Yes, moving north at one centimeter a year.
—You mean that where we're walking
was once in Tijuana?
—Just about. See there's granite here.
None just over the hill, she said.
—Oh, he said.
You mean those masks that look
like animals at a meeting?
—Yes, she said.
—Oh, he said.
Then a hole could open up right here,
a chasm we couldn't leap across?
She smiled,
—The fault's right up the strand there.

Wind and waves
fight eternally for control of the beach,
sea against land.

—Lots of people build on faults.
I used to live on one.
—How did it feel? he asked.
—No different from any other place.
Only you never knew
when you'd wake up

with your bed in your bathtub
and your bathtub
in your neighbor's garage.
—You think you're smart,
you know that, don't you?
She didn't answer him but kicked
beach sand savagely as they walked.

Sand piper runs ahead of wave,
leaps up when surprised,
follows wave out, picking, picking.

Running Away

I'll skip, I'll skip, with the jumping rope
I'll ride the merry train,
I'll trot away on the tumbleweed horse
But I won't come back again.

I'll run run run to the end of the road
Where the sky plummets down to the sea,
And I'll take my squirrel with me
Where the sky drops down to the sea.

I'll creak creak creak
Like a cricket in a crack
But I won't come back.

And he'll be sad when he finds me gone,
Because I've warned him times before,
If he didn't stop it I'd run away
To the land with the farthest shore.

I'll hit the dusty trail,
Slap, flap, with the flat of my feet.

I'll fly, I'll fly, over the highest hill,
Where the moon makes a hole in the sky,
And I'll take my squirrel with me,
Where the moon makes a hole in the sky.

I'll trot away on the tumbledown horse
I'll ride the merry train,
If my father ever spanks me any more,
I won't come home again.

Bicycle Morning Ride, Berkeley

When I pass by they make their obligatory
bark. Duty fulfilled, they snooze
till newsboys pitch willow arcs
onto second story balconies.

I take the same route daily, so
the dogs will get to know
me. How much I see
depends on my speed.
Some things I'd rather not, though
I get acquainted with a lot.

Black and brown women at the hills bus
transfer stop, wait for mistresses
who glide down in sleek cars to make
hurried pick-ups of their nannies.

Black and brown men at corners
waiting for the big stake trucks
and a job for a day, perhaps today.

I ride into the creeping sun, light
looking both ways, out and return,
familiar zig zag everywhere,
poetry of the day, harsh, glorious.

Streets a public dump, empty but
for the scum of night. Lovers
chippy out, leave droppings
of aluminum, paper, styrofoam
or wrinkled latex: fast foods,
fast friendships, fast folly.

Cats cry their way back into houses.

Her firm look as she bends to pick
up her paper with one hand, while the other,
casually gripping her robe, slips a little.
She never smiles, nor I, nor frowns.

She knows I will pass, I know she will bend.
She must know I can't stop. She is not
an early morning pick-up, though I'd swear
she times her bending to my pass.

Does her heart beat like mine
a little faster?

Heartbreak

Things in the heart get mixed up,
not orderly like romanesco broccoli,
more like poetry in a rain washed sky.

Some things you can't will your way,
like stop your heart from breaking.
Can't tell your heart: stop breaking, heart.

I know, I've tried. No triple by-pass,
angioplasty, no not nothing, any,
anything; down, down deviled down,
no way to will your way, none.

From the Wall at Angel Island
(a found poem)

Dear Lai-wah,

This is not Gold Mountain.

What we have found so far
has been rejection, insult, pain and misery.
We are treated like vermin by these White Devils.

They separate us, lock us up, question
our truth, even our sanity.

We are on an island. Our building
is large, there are bars and wire on windows.

At night, we can see the lights of land,
but we may never get there.

I am writing this letter—
others are writing poems—
to let the world know,
to leave in this place
something of me,
my mark.

Comfort Station #473-1

Comfort station
number four-seven-three dash one
is for me a Free Zone
for early morning fancy
in Lassen Volcanic National Park.

Its stately high seat
brings the ceiling down.
Colored light strains through.

My tinted pee beats pastel drops
from a tinted penis
against a tinted forewall.

Four-seven-three is a Siamese twin,
as water falling below
next door reminds me of our
joint disposal system.

I hear my neighbor
grunt and sigh and rain down pee.
This pleasing duet,
muted underground, is a
product of modern design
and a unisex morality.

I wonder what she thinks of me
as we struggle through our morning emptying.

O styrofoam and plastic wonder,
with your cement base
and translucent circle in your ceiling,
there is nothing natural about you
except us sitting, sitting.

Yet, since a morning seat
is for contemplation
not perturbation,
I salute you.

You furnish assembly line jobs
for workers in Torrance,
freight for Southern Pacific
and relief for us two.

Morning Mantra

Morning means re-ordering aches and grimaces.
Mostly it's swivel parts, like knees.
Four fingers of right hand hold my body

hostage. Pain streaks through them to neck
and the twitch in shoulder starts a dance.
Mind says, "Get up, get up. Six o'clock,

day's waiting." But body: "Hey, I need
a jump start a brand new heart. A pig's foot
and a bottle of beer or two" Unh unh, naw,

maybe an aspirin or so will have to do.
When I finish smiling at the silliness
in my life, false starts fizzled ends,

I stretch to see if back cooperates,
massage where it joins the rest of me,
Oooomm my morning mantra: Get your bottom up now,

get your bottom up, now. Despite the creak
of dry bones dry bones that know nothing
of *gentillesse*, I do.

The Passing of Kan Edo

The cat killed and ate a curious rat,
crunching bones, savoring them but leaving
entrails, serving notice to all who listen
that none need apply.

Hunger sated, the cat sat near the shoes,
looking up.

Ants began to crawl over what was left of rat.

Later the cat, after prowling the empty cupboard,
ran outside and let out a yowl.

Next day the neighbors, missing Kan Edo,
found his body sitting by his bed.

Chameleon

Mancha Cat
thinks he's a dog.
He will chase and fetch
fetch and carry
catch and carry.

He never misses

till he changes his mind.
Then he becomes a cat again
and ignores the toy I throw
as it soars over his head.

Looks at me as though he's
saying, "I'm a cat.
Didn't you know?"

CATTALK

Neighborhood cats hold their parliament
on the flat roof of our garage; it is
their throne room, their *sanctum sanctorum*

refuge from pine cones I throw
when they anoint my vegetable garden.
Early morning sun catches them

in their cleansing ritual, licking
away at legs and sides. The meow meows
congregate and a chicken wire fence

protects them. Heat inflames the tar and gravel.
Not a paw raised in dissent
as each adjourns to a corner in the shade.

Old Woman on the Basel Express

Fretting in and out of a bag
Too heavy for her age
She fidgets with her eyes even

Digging past neatly wrapped socks
And sweaters and drawers
She finds plastic-packed cottage cheese
Wax-papered wurst
And a giant natural banana

It seems bottomless, her bag

What is it she carries
Except what sustains her?
This smiling dwarf of a woman
On this speeding train.

Good Friday on Bear Valley Trail, 1978

25

Leaving the City
Is easy enough
Aim the car
Accelerate
Over the bridge

Escaping the City
Is something else
When I carry my desk
On my back
My head stuffed
With dates and digits

Takes awhile for the trail
To work its stimulation
Into the cracks and creases
Takes time for the earth
To come up and meet each step
Takes time for worry to wend its way
Down, down through the week's misery
Into the black clay and the small stones

On the trail
I meet my Shadow

Blossoms convert
Color for gloom
In quiet places
Yellow iris
Purple iris
Mestizo iris
A civil wilderness

Living is elimination
Of what is dead in me

Inspiration in hanging moss
And lichen centered on rock
Creating soil
Redemption in rhododendron

My eyes bounce
From dogwood
To alder and bay
And back and back

I smell the downed oak
Freshly cut legacy
Of the last storm

Will I need
To follow this trail
To where it ends
In the sea?

Will I need to wash
In its water
To be clean?

The Postman Rang For Us

He was "our" mailman.

Fifteen white folk worked
in the post office,
he the only colored
except the janitor.

No, he delivered mail to white folks, too.
He was making swings
when white men were in the back room
playing monopoly
and when they had retired
for the day.

Six straight times he was at the top
of the civil service list.
An Inspector had to come down
from Washington before they hired him.
Drew a government check then,
they couldn't mess with that.

Should think his wife would have been
proud of him, and perhaps she was.
But the man who ran the lumberyard
Got any woman in town he wanted
(or so it was said).

Beaten down by a mail sack
and a wife who cheated,
our mailman hung in his job,
whistled on his rounds,
sent a daughter away to college,
and basked in our praise.

The Gambler

You walk out the door
you take big chance,
I mean, you can be hit
by a car, mugged;
lots of crazies out there;
nothing, nobody's safe.

So I
put a buck or two now
and then on the lottery,
or go to Vegas once
in awhile
to yank the slots.

I know
what I'm doing. I'm taking
a chance. I know it,
win some lose some,
but what if I hit?

Set for life, not like
our streets where there's
no winners, stone cold
and set up for loss.

Walking Song

If you're walking along
and you meet someone
who is walking along,
say, "Good morning!"

If they're walking along,
they'll say, "Good morning!"

They'll say, "Good morning,
good morning." If they're
walking along they'll say,

"Good morning to you."

Poet Has Obscene Eye

Who Can Say Which Grain Will Grow

My mother ejected me
the day after she cleaned out a well.

I fell out running,
breath of hell at my back,
Sirocco, Mistral, Santa Ana in my face.
I had to learn to eat those winds,
to chill the devil's breath.

Midwife gazed at my third eye,
held my four hands in her own,
took fish from boats that were my feet.

"He shall sing." She said, examining
my vocal chords.

"But we need a cobbler, not a singer,"
my mother complained. "Singers
never eat well. Singers tell lies."

"He shall sing," cried the midwife,
"He shall sing."

How could I sing when I was not seen,
A toucan calling in the night?

What could I sing if I were not heard?

I ran up the wind and down the wind,
I sang to the wind, the wind carried my song.

I ran to the sun, I ran from the sun,
I sang to the birds, the birds carried my song.

Poet Has Obscene Eye

We have to show you
what we see, we scribblers.

Poet has an obscene eye,
Ferlinghetti knew it
Alta and Chaucer.

*I kan not gloss, I am
a rude man.* If she
pullen up her smock,
she pullen up her smock.

Pat Parker would get you
bad and down. Soyinka and
Tutuola did not hold
back for maids who blushed.

Pull the shade down any time
you wish. We are not nice.

Who would read us? How would
you know hell, heaven or the lands
between?

We are not pink, we poets,
we want to be read.

Refugees

Their frail housewares,
bed slats, pillows, chairs,
piled against the pole,
in the space between the sidewalk
and the street.

It was usable rubbish day.
The City's men would truck
it to the recycle yard.

Someone else had set it there,
as they could not.

Lived in that Section 8 apartment
around the corner.

I had only been gone a week.

Who had peeped to La Migra?

No more would I hear her shout
Callate! from that second story window.

No more musical language from kids
perennially at play in the stone yard
beyond my back fence. No more balls

to throw down from the garage,
or toys she trooped with them
around the block to retrieve.

They're in a holding facility,
their next door neighbor said,
before they send them back.

Back where? Those kids were born here.
I saw her bring the last one home
from County Hospital.

The neighbor mumbled something about
a new law, and turned away.

He would not look at me.

The Eye Behind the I

From here, I can go anywhere

Anchored to this desk, I see
three narcissus in a slender pewter vase

On the floor by my feet is my black bag
with its white clown faces,
empty now of my teaching tricks, it sags

French doors open out to campus
past trees, buildings, the town
out, out across the land

then up, up past clouds, up
out to the universe
planets, stars, galaxies, black holes

then I return, see again the desk
a highly glazed fat cup holds
pens that free my imagination

to soar   to soar

My Life is a Page

My life is a web page
My life is a web site
My life is a web

The web of my life is a page
yet unwritten. Who holds the pen,
who wields the strokes, round or slant,
rough or smooth?

Try as I may, and I try mightily,
every hour of every day to
unshackle my imagination,

Come on. Come on. Come on.
Hit me with heart hurt, blow hot
winds through me.

Let the hits light up the page
perforate the web.

The Hit

I have to write a thousand lines
for each ten I can keep.

In film work they shoot seven to get one;
one hit in three tries makes a fine hitter.

I should work where the odds
are not so long, you say, to sing my song.

Perhaps I would be a sweet swinger,
my stroke a thing of beauty;
or snap the picture
a thousand words can't match, natch!
Or maybe not be so fussy.

But when we scream in ecstasy
at the hit over the left field fence,
or admire the photograph on the gallery wall,
behind them are the wasted many thousands—

"Two thousand at bats," I
was told, "against big league pitching,
to become a hitter."

"For that one," she said, "That one on the wall there,
I don't know." And she waved her hands
in the direction of infinity.

So better for me I should stick to words,
be fussy, pick them clean and pick them fine.

At the Park

Yeats among his school children swings
gates open to endless speculation,
the child, man, forever questioning
what to know.

As the ball bounces, which is bouncer,
which is bounce?

We swing on a gateless gate, open,
open to a dark ring skittering,
skittering in the droppings of a bird.

Camus' Meursault and his sublime indifference,
equal to that of the universe,
S. Crane and his universe that did not care.
Equal to Macleish's tall tent, equal
to the roof of the world blown whoof.
A tiny rent in Christendom?

God!

The myriad ways of saying nothing,
nothing, nothing…nothing at all.

After Forgetting Lines of Two Poems

Can Eagles dance?

Can I in long bones leap?

My hands are shaking now,

calling the direction of my brain

into question. A shaking hand,

long bones leaping, an eagle

dancing. Why not fly, eagle,

leave us who have

no wings, who drag our bodies

through the dry seasons,

to flutter our ghosts.

The Garden

Full of Flying Things

in the spirit of Tz'u

The air is full of flying things,

birds flying. Air is full

of flying birds, birds flying.

The air is full of falling leaves,

leaves falling. Air is full

of flying geese, geese calling.

Wild geese call, shadows fall,

wine flows under moon.

Wild geese call, the lovers part,

fill the wine cup one more time.

Break their hearts, their lives will start,

shadows fall, wild geese call.

Guanajuato Birds Return at Evening

They hit the eye
as a black point
on the high horizon.

A wedge expands and folds,
a headless snake, body fattened,
airborne, sweeping mightily.

Sweep, sweep and counter sweep,
wheeling *abamicos*; heavy wind,
they hurtle with seeming mindlessness,
hit the ear like wind pushed rain.

Thousands, so close, yet with bird radar,
never touching, wave after wave,
they make the inestimable pass,
pass and pass again.

Black punctured cloud.

Their timing immaculate, ten of six
each night, rush of bird of blood.
Branch sagging numbers, they settle,
chattering, chattering, safe for now
in Embajadora's trees.

The Garden

There is satisfaction in turning earth,
A measured amount to accomplish,
One forkful at a time,
Preparing a place to plant.

Adds up before you know it:
Earth turned, composted, weeds under,
Muscling the fork in, quick twist of the wrists
You can see what you've done.

Earth's there to receive the seed,
Nothing abstract or subjective, no caprice.
The judgment of the land is absolute.
Just running sweat under the sun
And a prayer for cooling rains.

Note to an Aspiring Gardener

Dear Luke,

More than water and sweat,
more than a green thumb,
ducks that catch snails,
chickens that shit between rows,
I don't know what it takes, Luke;

God's blessing, moon
in right place, wife's
menstrual blood?

You've gotten books: *Better
Homes and Gardens, Grow
Your Own and Like It*—
you tell me.

Why don't you sleep out there
and try talking to them, Luke?
That's it, talking to them,
talking to them, just
talking to them. Sleep out there,
Luke, and try talking to them.
That ought to do it just fine.

Your soil brother,

Clem.

Apocalypse is My Garden

The breaking up
and down of things

Sitting on a lava block, this rock,
a reminder that other times meant other things.

While farmers in Europe plowed their land,
that was not theirs to waste with ruin,
Lassen erupted and for seven years
the mountain shook.

The world shook.

Europe stayed revolution by starting
a war. What revolution had earth planned?

The mountains just needed to break out,
magma jetted through vents skyward,
plague of flowing stone and fire,
incinerated cedar and redwood,
tephra cone volcanoes,
flaming rocks and mushroom clouds,
house-sized boulders tossed
on Devil's Postpile, re-shaping
land, raising here, leveling there.

Tehama, an acid factory, burbling
under our feet, sulphur and nitrate explosions,
smell of grey scent, rotten eggs.

Embedded in lava pockets, squirrel scat,
staghorn lichen, seeds and dust.

A rain and something new will grow.

Yucca

Our lone yucca blossomed the year
of the heavy wet. Basement

flooded, storm drain clogged
sidewalk blocked by restraining wall

and there stood the yucca blooming.

Since the yucca doesn't bloom every year
its birthing is an event:

sulky, brown tipped, squat, solidly
among the wild blackberries; porcupine

bristling, claiming and protecting that
dark corner of the garden. Its cohorts

borage and a curling vine I've found
no name for, all are pressed down

by the rains. I respect its space
having no other choice.

Above all that gloom
shoots the green yucca
blossoming white.

Weeding

Weeding is satisfying
Selecting what
Is a matter of definition

Oxalis brightens the dull greens

Despite the rigor in tending
The robust remain

I don't want to eradicate anything
Willing to just pull some
No campaign of extermination
I want to achieve a balance
A kind of live and let live

Glad to have the beets bump bottoms
With wild onions
Strength through osmosis
Oregano rub leaves with summer savory

If the pesky dandelion would hold
Her gold for one minute more!

"A weed is a flower out of place"
A gardener is a banker
Out of season

Patterns on the Angled Stones

A slug appeared on a toadstool
Near the bottom of the walk this morning
Grey trail glistening on the black stones
Making angled patterns on the angled stones
A slug appeared on a toadstool
After last night's rain

Big slug
They tell me if I put salt on your tail
You'll vanish
Slug, you tell me, as I work my magic
Is your tail the direction you're going
Is your tail the direction you're coming from?

Now I've got nothing against slugs
You're like a lot of other lives
That hurry in and out like moths
Reaching for light after rain

Only, the slug drags his memory
And leaves it glistening on the cobblestones
An angled pattern on the angled stones

Scar

When I see trunks of majestic trees
gouged with initials, even those of lovers,
my hackles rise.

Though I know they mean no harm,
shackled by love and the wish to let us know,
or need to leave a notice: *Kilroy was here.*

Dogs raise their hind leg and squirt a memoir,
birds leave droppings, as do hens,
but these are ephemera, returning to earth
and air, they leave no lasting scar.
These other, these blade slash reminders
grow with the tree, etched-in wantonness.

Do we need to scar to remember?

Recipe, a Love Poem

Prepare the garden
Open the earth gently
Stroke the land under the hand
Finger the body for seed

Tend the garden
Spade deep, thin out plums, weed tomatoes
The push and pull of succulent motions
Asparagus sucking

Seek not goal but process
Repetition and renewal
In the garden
Plucking the body's lyre

Fondle the soft surfaces, peaches, apricots
Our only crime can be
The acceptance of cruelty
An ignorance of berries and of beets

Women at the Fence, at the Well

to Sandra Bond Garrison

Women who stand at fences
stand together and apart.

Their fence is separation, not a wall.

Women who stand at fences channel
love through hands that pass
the trowel, tulips, tea roses,
bleeding hearts and tansy,
pass their hands over and back;
tea roses, talk of chrysanthemums, tea talk,
ritual turn of phrase, twist of hand fork,
honeysuckle on one side, jasmine on the other.

They trade stories of success and sorrow.
Feeling flows between the lines,
crone lines of courage and gentleness.
Two crones, fingers in earth, exchange
secrets of bulbs, ladybugs. Their stories
hold no bitterness.

Anchor Steel links let light through;
not like love or plants, they need no tending.
Women go to the well for water, the fence
to freshen the spirit.

Women who stand at fences
stand together and apart.
Their fence is separation not a wall.

Night Work

Middle of the night
When police are out chasing thugs
And in other ways keeping the peace,
I've got my flashlight
Playing cops and robbers
With snails and slugs
And cut worms that get bold.

I could use spray, they tell me,
And some other poisons,
Wipe 'em all out
Or pellet bombs; they eat them and explode.

But I don't want to do that.

Don't want to take no part
In no micro-decimation
With dead snails around
For a generation of birds to peck
Or the neighbor's cat.

No.

I'd rather take my chances on missing some
Bending eyeball to snail ball
Fingering the slime of slugs
Ker Plump! into bio-degradable suds
Then the earth
To start over.

My Garden Lovers

Why do weeds entangle flowers?
Extricate them gently
As they clutch.
Too often weeds and flowers
are look-alikes. Yank one
you get them both.

Are the weeds asking,
Why pull me?
as they grip tighter.
I belong here too.

*Why not my friend
the poppy?*

Out you invader, I answer.
I extricate them gently
as they cling.

You have got to go.
No way I'm going
to let you stay.

But a wee thought
twiggles my mind,
What if the flower
invited the weed,
that the one
seeks the other?

Ode to the Hachiya Tree

O Bountiful, your ample roundness thrills me.
You are not slender graceful like the cedar,
Nor majestic like the great oak,
nor would I want you to be.
I could never reach your goodness.

You are just the right shape:
The matter for nut bread, pudding, a drink so rich
its delight resonates.

From the tips of your branches your fruit hangs,
on this twig this sprig of skinny through the eye
of a needle branch this heaviness. I marvel at your
knowledge, that you can hold it as it puffs out and
rounds, changes color from shades of green to,
well, persimmon.

There you are, holding fruit,
leaves like sails shielding it from thieving eyes,
beast or human.

Not a thousand strong, like my neighbor Kan Edo's,
maybe fifty in a good year, birds and squirrels willing.
But Oh that fifty, great glowing grand, you must be
boastful proud my friend my tree.

•

You have gone.
Your gorgeous leaves, where are they now, your fruit,
the monster slurp, no shade in dry season no
sun in wet.

You live now only in my memory of seasons past,
of you as a sproutling, sickly, our struggle to make
you grow, become a tree. With care you thrived
Bountiful, filled out and gave and gave.

Now you are no more.

Gone from this wretched place that we call earth,
this wobbly shaky, this bumbly boodlestump.
Do you know as I feel that this season may be our last?

Forever Afternoon

What is death to the caterpillar
we call a butterfly
— anonymous

Ladder of success is an image I abhor.
I prefer the double helix, intertwining spirals.

My spirit does not wear down
or wear out, like a car or a shoe.

While my body wanes, waxes my spirit
brighter.

I am in eternal metamorphosis.
Constantly consumed,
I consume myself.

Life has no stages; the word resolution
lies; life has questions, connections.

Life is a wheel of fortune, my life
a gift to be passed around the wheel.

Do we ask where does the caterpillar
go when it becomes a butterfly?

The caterpillar does not go, it becomes.

Spirit of caterpillar lives in butterfly,
same heart, beating stronger.

The Geese are Back!

after reading Tz'u

After the last wild storm
heaved itself over the mountain,
geese came back.

High flying geese, welcome.

Where have you been, geese?
How long will you pleasure us
with your presence?

We've been waiting all year
for your return. When you fly away
the marsh is lonely. Other birds
visit, we're glad to receive them.
They, too, have their place in the chain.

But it is not the same, geese. You,
with your grand honk, your stentorian
call, bring a calming certainty
to the cycle of fly away and return.

Sunshine Wash

Thanksgiving at Point Reyes

My mother liked to wash
In the Big Water
At sunrise
Before she had to go to work
Or the white folks came.

"Can feel my changes better,"
She'd tell me, I,
Dog paddling from root to root,
Eyes wary for water snakes,
Was not impressed by her ritual.

The awe falls now
As I think my life
Under the sound of green waves
On this western shore
The cold sun low
Against the bright land.

While I Thought God, My Mother Saw

61

While I thought God, my mother saw.
She worked, watched and prayed
"living humble," knowing the bell
had rung.

"Rock" to my mother was a place to hide.
While I, ignorant though not innocent of sin,
played "can't ketch me"
around the huge stone in the lower yard.

My mother's hell was a fiery furnace,
rock-melting hot,
a vision she wanted me to share.

God knows I tried. But at twelve I found
her longing for my salvation
a burden too great to bear.

When she cried, "Jesus, Jesus," I fell outside
her pain and ecstasy, as she walked
and talked with The One who gathered her
in His arms and saw her home.

My Trip

My trip begins
in a slender house
in a thick wood.

Weak light
guides the midwife
as she pulls me out.

Grandma Ozelia shouts,
"Praise the Lord!"

Then grandma's farm
its cows, pigs, the mule,
and my rabbit
suffocates
under a pile
of barnyard lumber.

Aunts and uncles
who tend me
when my mother
has to leave
my father,
and who are soon to join
the 20's Migration
North.

"Snake holes"
to stand over,
my first punishment
for theft, of my
youngest uncle's
elderberry wine.

Then the small town,
many houses, each
we live in for
far too short a time.

My sisters' books
from school
amo, amas, amat,
they practice
their Latin lessons
on four-year-old me.

The pre-Depression
store we own
one winter;
my stepfather
gives credit
to his friends
despite my mother's
warning, then
sawmill whistle
lays them all off.

On railroad tracks
kerosene holder
for kitchen stove
drops and smashes
while moving
to cheaper house;
no money
to replace.

Barefoot to negro school,
white children torment us
as we pass their place;

never to use public
library or any
tax-supported
leisure space;
bright enough
to sense a wrong.

Work from age nine
like my buddies
at odd jobs
after school, weekends.

Eleven-year-old
favorite sister dies;
why, why, why?

Good times, eating
hot candied yams,
butter dripping,
stone-ground
whole wheat rolls
from government issue
flour, a puppy
one whole summer long.

Reading books,
winning a bible verse
contest at ten.

Mulatto-run House
for white men
down the street
where I make
good money
shining shoes;
madam mistress
to police chief.

Falling from
every ladder,
fence or tree
I climb, yet
forever climbing.

"That boy live
to see twelve
will be a miracle,"
my mother swears.

I do live
and in my most
Jesus voice
announce:
"I must be about
my Father's business,
now that I'm twelve."

"You better sit down here
and eat your dinner
before it gets cold.
Father's business
my big foot."

A prophet is never
received well
in his own country,
I remind her.
Like the Rock of Ages
She can not
be moved.

My Dog When I Was Seven

The year was 1930
When my family produced nothing
To add to the GNP

Out of the money economy
We were both underfed and skinny-legged

He came in from the street
I fed him part of what I had
The rest he scrounged in outhouses
Reached before the city's honeybucket men.
He drank from a scum-filled ditch
At the bottom of our yard

My buddy

We ran up the dirt sidewalk a way
Then back home
I was happy to have someone my own size

That day in July his eyes took fire
Foam at the mouth, his piteous yelps
As he zigzagged through his madness

At the end,
Body caked with dust and sweat
His coat a mud gray, he lay, teeth bared
In a hideous stiffness

My stepfather warned "don't touch"
But through my tears buried him
Where he lay

Origin obscure, ancestry uncertain, pedigree none
I didn't keep him long enough to name.

Night on the Town

Public space belonged to white folk.
Big black folk knew this and cleared
out of it at night. Little black folk
didn't know it yet, and, by keeping quiet,
slipped under the radar of whites' scorn.

"Cute little nigger," they sometimes said,
They gave me a penny as they rubbed my head.
(Lore had it that "rubbing a little nigger's head"
made dice fall seven-eleven. A *little* nigger.)

We had no electric lights where we lived,
the nearest were five blocks away
on a white people street. So, for me,
sneaking into bright downtown at night
was like creeping from a deep forest
into a savanna. Lions and leopards
may lurk there, but oh, how gaudy!

My mother knew about public space.
Her "Stay out from under white folk's feet"
circled between my ears on warm nights when
I wandered streets where lighted windows
held electric trains perpetually
entering and exiting tunnels,
scoop that swung down, picked up sand,
dumped it on red truck's flat bed,
then swung back for more.

I feel a rip at my shoulder as a finger pulls at
an unmended tear in my shirt. I see a reflection
of two white men behind me. My older sister works
after school for one man's wife, cleaning,
washing and ironing clothes by hand,
handing her things she can well get herself.
I do not think he knows me, but I see him
evenings when I go to their house
to walk my sister home.

I feel hot air, hear laughter
as they walk away, turn to see one
punching the arm of the other.

"You are eight years old," I can hear my mother
through my tears. "You old enough to know right
from wrong. How many times have I got to tell you,
stay out of them streets at night. You know I got
no money to buy thread to fix that shirt."

I look around at the big white people with their
families. They look at me with sympathy, turn
quickly away, grip the hands of their children
tighter.

My Mother Washed Other People's Clothes

Sometimes I feel I handwash clothes
to be near my mother

I feel her blood pulsing
through mine as I press down
and pull up, press and pull, scrubbing

Sometimes I work the board
but mostly I use my fingers
press and pull our arms and shoulders

She scrubbed that we could eat

How she stood it when the trapped blond
pushed her. We are both pushed. She
by the blond, I by my desire to excel

I could pay someone, or
take clothes to the laundromat but
I love the smell of sunshine wash

In some things I take the easy way
but when I want to feel my mother
I have to slip into her rhythm

The blond boss lady was expected not to work
but to direct folk like Mama, Southern and black
before the Civil Rights Revolution

It was not a job my mother loved
She was a people not a thing person
(who aspired to nursing)
and she had us four to feed

Through the grey weather the line of clothes
was never clean, never dry enough. She heated
the smoothing iron on coals never hot enough

Their ashes smudged some things. "That woman's
whine drive me crazy," my mother would tell us
"Husband this and husband that. *Beats me for*

nothing when he comes in from the mill. Says
she gets back at him but don't say how."

Mama was a small woman
and the iron was heavy

She talked to my older sister, who was twelve,
of a juicy roundness, destined too soon to go
North, mind babies, cook hash, learn the word
schwartze

Told her to hold on

We pulled together with the quarter
from the lawn I mowed, my sister's seventy-five
cents for a week's work after school

That's what we had
that and my mother's pride

I love the smell of sunshine wash
and I feel my mother
as I squeeze it out

Night Trip Downtown

When I am nine
my mother despairs
of my staying put
anywhere, except behind
a ball and chain.

*Keep out of the streets
at night.* I don't hear her.
*And don't let me catch you
downtown.*

House is no place
for anyone on hot steamy night.
Downtown is where store
windows glitter.

Toy crane swings, its scoop
reaches out, closes over
gravel, lifts, swings
back to pile, empties
and returns.

Sunday-dressed white people
pause, look briefly,
pass on. As long as
I don't move, or speak,
they will not see me.

It grows late,
the crowds thin.

*Come over here, boy,
I got something for you.*

He stands across the narrow street,
right hand on a crutch, his left
jingling coins in his pocket.

His voice has gravel in it.

I do not know him,
not a white man I have seen
on my shoeshine rounds.

*Come on over here, I'm not
going to hurt you.* This when
I hesitate. He starts to cross
over, his crutch makes a klock,
klock, klock as he advances.

I edge away, he wheedles,
I move faster, start to run.
Turning the corner I hear,
…little black bastards downtown.

Shorty the Iceman

I was a summer idler, Friday,
watching the blocks of ice crash klunking
out of the metal chute,
to the waiting grappling hooks,
as a man slid it along the floor,
with a cruump into a waiting wagon.

"Boy, you want to work for me?"
He was the one they called Shorty, walked
with a limp. A summer job!

"All you got to do is take the ice in,
put it in the ice box. I'll pick it."

"Yes, sir. But I'll have to ask my mama,
if I'm gonna be working all day."

"All right. You akx your momma. Give
you fifty cents week. You any good,
make it a dollar. Be here Monday mornin."

"I don't know anything about this Mister Shorty,"
my mother was her usual skeptical self when I showed
enthusiasm over any new venture (she was usually right).
"But I guess it'll be better than hanging around
that old ice house. Worse yet, out in the streets."

Monday morning early I was there
while Shorty was backing Evelyn
into her traces. She was brown, alert, benign.
Gave a nod in my direction. I went to pet her.
"Leave that mule alone. I need you t'hep me.
Come on hep me wit this ice." He was
struggling to arrange the hundred-pound blocks
in the wagon. I was slightly built, underweight
for my age; he didn't get much help from me.

Besides, my job was to begin when the wagon
was loaded and ready to roll. All the other
helper boys were standing around,
waiting for their drivers to call them.

Shorty's route was through a mainly white section
of town, large, well-kept houses, colonial-styled
white columns, with long shaded driveways
to the screened-in back porches, where the ice boxes
were located. Evelyn knew the route, Shorty knew
each house's daily order. Once in a while
a cook would send me back to the wagon for
"another twenty-five pounds if you got it.
We be having a party tonight."

Schooled by my mother to be polite to my elders,
and to move quickly when I worked, "none of that
slouching off there," I quickly became a favorite
with the cooks and maids on our route.

"Sonny Boy, you want a piece of this pie?"
I never had to be asked twice. "Now don't
let Shorty see it. He'll want some, and
he ain't getting none."

Nickels, a rare dime, many slices of potato pie
and deep-fried chicken drumsticks were
my fringe benefits.

I wanted to share with Shorty, another part
of my mother's schooling, "Don't be greedy now,"
but something in the cooks' warning made me
hold back. I pocketed my tips and ate my
yum yums on the long driveways back to the wagon.

Miss Bronson, my fifth grade teacher, was working
as a maid that summer, when she was supposed
to be in "New Yawk." She answered the door

as I was delivering their ice. She didn't need to tip
the dime (twice what anyone on the street gave)
to insure my silence. Her face as she opened
the door did that.

Our days were hot. Though our route wound
through tree-lined streets, making it cooler
than some, we were sweating by ten o'clock.
By noon our backs were soaked. Shorty's
limp became more noticeable as the day
grew hotter. He became irritable with Evelyn,
hitting her with a long cane if she stopped,
when a simple shake of the reins would have moved her.
I remembered the difference between the way
my uncles Ben and Johnny handled their mules,
Ben being the short-tempered one, going
for the whip at the least sign of a balk.

Using a grappling hook, Shorty positioned
the large blocks, and used an ice pick
to separate them into the weights each house needed.
I put the ice into a canvas bag that I slung over
my shoulder. Most orders were for fifteen
or twenty-five pounds, weights I could handle.

As the days passed, I sensed that Shorty
was looking to find something wrong with
my work. If a driveway was particularly long,
he would sometimes move to our next stop
without waiting for me. "We ain't got all day
you know," when I ran panting to catch up.
Determined to give Shorty nothing to find fault
with, I tightened up the time I used
for each delivery. This way
the week passed quickly, with no
further reprimand from him.

Each day I took my tips
home. By week's end they totaled a dollar
seventy-five cents. With my pay, I could buy
a pair of new secondhand shoes for school.
Had seen just the pair I wanted in Silver's window.

Saturday afternoon the helper boys gathered
around their drivers to receive their pay.
There was a lot of good-natured banter
between them. "What I'm o pay you for? Jivin
all them cute cooks and maids on the route.
Don't lie, now, I seed you. You ought to be payin
me."

I didn't see Shorty among the other drivers.
"He over there," one of the men told me,
when I asked for him. He was standing near
the barn. "I'd like to get on home now, Mr.
Shorty. Appreciate that little change."
"Boy, I ain't got nothin for you. You know
they took a lot out of my pay envelope
this week. I come up a little short."

I was stunned.

No money? I couldn't buy my shoes.
They cost two-seventy five. I was counting
on a dollar because he hadn't found
anything wrong with my work.

I looked over at the crowd of other drivers
and their helpers. They had stopped their
banter to pay attention to us.

When I recovered sufficiently, I asked him,
"When you go pay me?"

The other drivers started laughing. "Shorty,
he don't pay nobody. Be a fool to work for Shorty."

"Naw, he'll pay you. He just want you to beg
him for it. Then he'll throw it on the ground."

I looked at Shorty, standing there, jingling
coins in his pocket. The others looked to see
what I would do.

At first I didn't believe them.
How could he, how could anyone,
not pay me till I had begged
for my money. They were joking,
had to be.

But, looking at Shorty standing there,
jingling coins, I knew they weren't.

My mother hadn't raised me to beg. I mean,
from nobody. The money, keep it. I started
to walk away.

"Boy, you ain't going to walk off and leave
your money like that." "I wouldn't let him…"
I kept walking. My mother said mark it up
to experience. "I didn't figure that little
cripple nigger was no good nohow."

Sunday Visit to a Carolina Chain Gang

Nobody works on Sunday, we were a Christian nation,
we kept the Lord's day sacred, even here.

The men lay around, most chained to a low standing
bar that ran the length of the camp. Others sought shade
where they could find it, within

the watchful eye of the white man with a comfortable belly
and a double-barreled shotgun. Two bloodhounds slept
under a small tree on his right.

I played marbles with myself while my stepfather talked
with one of his buddies, to whom he'd brought some chicken,
rice and a slice of pound cake Mama made.

 "Don't run off now," he shot over his
shoulder, as I chased my favorite taw
down a slight incline.

Heard a man comin', comin' soon," his buddy said.
"Take most of these, I don't know where,
Georgia, 'labama, down that way.

Hear they got steel mills, factories an' like that.
Anybody got no job got to go. Had a job last week,
don't count. Got to have a white man say you
workin' for him now, right now."

I spotted a boy not much older than I, lying
At the edge of shade as the sun moved,
he had stretched as far as his chains allowed.

I started over to him to see if he could play.
"Get back there!" the white man shouted,
the camp aroused, men stood, rattled their chains;
the dogs alert, stiffened. My stepfather ran to me,
pulled me back to where we'd been.

"You better go, man. You know how
things get when Charlie revved up."

"Can't take you no place," my
stepfather chided, as he half dragged
me after him.

Graduation

There was a space in the front of my mouth
where a new tooth should have been. Dr. D
would have replaced it had school closed
when they said it would.
But the polio epidemic pushed everything up.
We let school out three weeks early.

I don't remember what I said,
after their laughter, so spontaneous
as to seem planned. Welcome is what
the Salutatorian gives. That was me,
and welcome was what I attempted.

"I greet you all…" *"Hahaha! Hahaha…"*
The front rows began it and the other rows
joined in. I heard my voice but I could not hear
what I was saying. Something about
joy in friendship.

These were my classmates? These were they
whom I'd sat next to in rooms, played
with in yards, one of whom I thought
I was in love with? Was she
there among the laughers? Then one
reared back in her seat and swung up
her heels. I remember a scarlet slip
and yellow shoes. Yellow patent leather
shoes moving up and down, up and down.

Woodshedding

> "Is that all, are you *through?*"
> —Ruby

How can I send back
that look of scorn?

"The *big* boys know
how to do it."

Wasn't *I* a big boy?
I was fifteen.

Didn't I do what
the big boys said?

Even, "Love her up
and be sure you
put it on *before*
you put it in."

Their advice burned
in my brain, as her eyes
scorched my shriveled self.

Not their words, I had
followed them

to a tee. No,
it was me, alas.

No question of a
second chance, those

eyes for many years
would make me
fumble every pass
that came my way.

Torn Shirt in Kingston, Jamaica

He has on that shirt I saw,
worn and frayed, in Lagos,
the small boat at Yeji,
Turkish quarter in Grenoble.

I fold a ten dollar bill
tuck his fingers around it:
"Take this to your mother,
Tell her
get you a new shirt."

He takes the bill and runs.

What he thinks of me,
my distress,
his eyes don't tell.

What I want
to tell myself is,
let it go, let it go.

I am a small eight,
window shopping
summer Sunday evening,
straight down town
where white folk go.

Warned but won't listen.

See reflected
a moment
two men
pass behind me,
feel quick pull in soft cloth,
more sticky air,
hear laughter.

My hot tears.

No way my mother
can repair
that fresh rip.
Needle but
no thread,
no money.

Let it go, now.
Let it go.

A Hole in My Night

There's a hole in my night
and the wind is screaming.

I've been trying to plug that hole
but the moon ain't right.

There's a hole in my night.
Not the kind that sheep race through;
it's bigger than that.
I pull down my hat,
put hands to my ears
to block out the screams.

Keep telling myself
I must be dreaming.
Wake up in the morning,
hole's not there.
My days are whole,
but there is a hole, a hole, a hole,
a hole in my night.

Why I Hurry

When I hurry, things I haven't learned,

or not learned well enough, get in

my way, fall down, rise up, run in,

run out, throw road blocks, create

bottlenecks, logjams, drag me through

quicksand, a maze.

But I *must* hurry.

I don't see no time sitting around

waiting for me, holding no gate open

with no oud trio, making no bow

saying: take your time, old man

you got all of me in the world.

Love Poem

We don't have to plan love.
It is in our talk
of vacuum cleaning
or fixing a zipper.

Loving is not to break stride
but to do what there is to do.
We don't have to work at love
but at cooking dinner
and hanging the wash.

Exchanging events in our lives,
we do what we do
as we do it, as natural as breathing.
You smell like sunshine wash.
Sunshine turns me around
and around and around.

Conjures

The Hungry Black Child

lord

forgive me

if I twist the sunset

but when evening twist my belly

i see red

walking the field the woods

the houses on my street

white

burning burning

What They Say, What I Saw

Before I went to Africa I read
the names of people and things.
The map, alas, is not the territory.

They say huts, I saw houses,
small, round, pointed, square.
They say bush, I saw tall grasses
and shrubs, that fed and sheltered
beasts and birds.
I saw forests where they said jungle,
deep, warmly dark, flashes of sun
on their rivers, noisy with monkeys and birds.
For Bushmen, I saw Dan people,
for tribe I saw Kingdom, of the Yoruba,
Dahomey, Ashanti, Benin.

The British told the Ibo,
"Take us to your leader."
"Leader?" the Ibo asked,
and just laughed.

Mission

For Malcolm X, MLK, Jr., Robt. Kennedy, Geo. Jackson, Viola Liuzo
and all those others killed the moment they got it together.

When you speak
For those ground between gears
Who drag the earth in their pockets
And eat poor
You step out on point
Into an ambush
Certain as the day is long.

Those who nourish
The earth with their blood
Those who fall rising
Will praise you
And send you their love.

But unless my scouting reports are wrong
Or I've missed a briefing
Turn your eyes this way and that way
When you offer yourself
And weigh the crossfire well.

Free Way

They were a destination only to their friends;
to others, they were on the road to somewhere
from somewhere else.

They had saved and bought, grounded them-
selves in a section of town few wanted then,
like that Navajo/Hopi land
over the coal and uranium.

They lived in houses hardly seen by us
who groused that SLOW signs arrested
our flight toward the new bridge.

Faded off-white, some in need of paint,
paid for with earnings from Second World War,
scorched metal dollars from hot holds of ships.

Yes, they were not a destination.

Ella Grandison was lured there while her
Isaac helped build the Burma Road. More
money than for Negroes in Texas.

This modest home was their stake in the world.
Children raised on potatoes, butter beans,
collard greens. Not warm enough for okra.

Would the Grandisons and their neighbors be able
to afford a house with land for the money
the white state would force them to accept?

Would their new place be a destination?

Planes of View

after Hurricane Katrina

A

I built my house where I shouldn'ta
'cause I couldn'ta built it nowhere else.
Now the flood done come and took it,
like they knew it would.

When they picked us up off of the roof,
me and my parrot, they made me leave
him behind.

Boat ain't no place, them people say,
For no squawkin' bird.

Henry was some *good* company,
the best I had.

        B

        We sent out two plane loads
        to San Diego and San Francisco,
        twin giant hollow birds jammed with
        our dogs and cats. This while
        bodies floated like bundles
        bounding gently in the toxic gumbo,
        and that one over in Algiers lay
        soaking up sun and fetid air.

        I helicoptered over the shifting scene.

        These were folks I had seen
        sitting on stoops, groups idling at corners,
        never amounted to much. Oh,
        those little ones, childr—

        We even got out one parrot.
        Ungrateful bird. Here we were
        rescuing him, and all he could crack
        was, *Goddamn your souls to hell!*

West African Woman Casts Her Shadow

Raise and lower, rise and fall
The rise and fall of the pounding stick
Market bought or homemade
Classroom for your daughter and her friends
My Mother
Lift and pound, lift and pound
Change hands, shift the baby

How long do you stand here, or sit there?
My first image, strong in the eye
The mind, fixed in time
How long are you wedded to the pounding stick?

Into the pestle go all the short and long dreams
The yam crop, the plantain, groundnut, the red bra
The weight of the child you carry

You may not tire, you cannot grow old

The world grows old

Your men leave or they die
Your daughters pick up their sticks while you still live
Their rhythm, your rhythm
You, my Mother, your rhythm feeds us
Makes the cycle of our days, our seasons
While you know no day, no night
No season

You awake in the dark, feel
Your way into the sun
The fields beckon, morning chores aside
The shop beckons the stall beckons
The load for your head must be made ready
The arrangement just so, the cloth shifted,
Onto the back the child

Your rhythm feeds us, makes the cycle of our days
Our seasons
You may not grow old, you may not tire
Life eternal is your dominion

In the many tongues, pimpim-pimpim
Pimpim-pimpim, lift and smash
Raise and lower, shift the weight you carry
Look up
Stride your way into the sun
Walk a fine, my Mother, walkafine

Mother Images

Sweet potatoes: yam smacking bam lips
sweet tasting good.
Standing at the stove, over the ironing board,
sitting with a lap full of snap peas,
shelling peas, snapping fresh corn in two quick
violent motions, deft, practiced
cutting up apples, peeling pears, ripping skin
off beets.

Skinning a rabbit, beheading and gutting
a fish, disemboweling a chicken,
heads chopped, rolled,
barnyard and kitchen violence.

Knife under gills, towards eyes,
slice down on neck. Filet
knife against the spine, edge between flesh and spine,
work down slowly.

How many chickens scalded, peas shelled,
beans snapped, hoe cakes flipped,
fish scaled, yams baked, biscuits punched,
pots stirred? How many tears shed over onions—
how high a pile would it make?

These murderous actions are daily, continuous
at the apex of the food chain, ritualized
in our house, down the street,
across town, around the world.
Hands of women make killing arcs
so that they and their own
can live.

Thoughts On My Return From the Caribbean

> *O never to be far from*
> *the sight and sound of the sea.*
> — Tourist

> *I like the sight and sound of money.*
> — Resident

When heat seeps through my bones,
when stories rear from peopled islands
of past lives and present troubles,
I hate the cruelties of travel.

I hate the heaviness of beach hotels
that anchor bays and press locals
to rent their time
and bodies for food.

I walk streets, look into eyes most tourists shun,
eat where Jimmy Cliff wails "Viet Nam, Viet Nam"
on a cassette player, ride buses jammed
with bodies, baskets, mothers with babies,
hear ancient Scottish sounds in the soft dark
and know I'm in "Little England."

Stands to scan the sea, cement houses
poured against lush hills, havens
from those who live below.
                    Travelers go
not to see the rattrap shacks of the quaint
boys who catch their coins, or
gigolos who catch their women, or
crew quarters of their floating palaces.

I am drawn to the islands, where spice trees
replace manioc for dollars for bread.
Harbor boys long to follow the bananas, coffee,
where the big boats go. Sometimes they do.

One-shirt boys, these young soldier men:
afro black, latino black, francophone,
march blind, run blind in their first boots,
chanting "Government Boots, Government Boots!"
with vain dreams of their day in power.

Though I am glad to be home from the Islands,
where people migrate one to another if
there may be more food and better work,

where leaders are loathed and feared,
backed by guns exchanged
for their lands' goods and their pride,

where artists are important once they're praised
by those outside, the rich won't be shown
the crooked path their money has traveled,
where those who can, leave,

I will go back to the Islands.

My people were brought through there.
I'm hooked on the stories their people tell.

High Brown, High Sorrow

In Xhosa a young girl is a spring field

to Janice Washington

I

Your history is long in our lands
Names for you are legend
They all say 'hybrid' not 'human'.

A slavemaster bedded a slave
The fateful crossing began.

Warp and woof of night acts,
genes flowed over racial lines and back.
You had to be accounted for. They said:
"The mother swallowed a frog, ha! ha!"

II

Your history is long in our lands.
Eyes green, grey, brown, you've
had to take the measure of our fantasies.
Object, thing, divine creature in our sight.
Object of our lust we never let you rest,
object of our dreams we never let you sleep.

Your real self down too deep to reach,
you plumb the depth of our racial curse.
In languages that clutterfy our own,
you learn to make do and do well.

III

It is not simply we would make you
our trophy, wear you on our ring finger,
round our necks, hang you from an ear;
stand you frozen in a case for gawkers,
as Norwegians once did their Northern kin,
and as we did Ota Benga.

We would break you if we could. We humans
create our gods. What we worship we destroy
as well. When blocked, we smash our idols
and regenerate their dust.

In Xhosa a young girl is land in the spring
after rain breaks the drought.
The Xhosa know. Do you know
that you are land in the spring,
rain that slakes the drought?
Is the secret of your power
what you know?

Coast Castle Dungeon, Slave Coast

I

When this castle was new, the floor of this dungeon
was clean smoothed rock. Now three feet of bloodsweat
soaked earth from the thousand plus thousands feet
holds chicken bones, mouth picks, combs and what none
can say.

Those days were sunny too.
Mango groves grew down to water's edge.
Fisher people pushed their bright-prowed pirogues
into the surf; they push them now.

II

Did they hide when they spotted the slavers,
was there panic or crafty watching,
marvelling at how the blocky craft stayed afloat?
When it stopped moving,
they were certain it would sink.

How long did they wait from the first speck
till the forest of sails dropped anchor?

They did not know the spyglass
that caught the sun's light
jeweled flecks, saw
better than their eyes,
that distance was no savior from sight.

Was it gods or devils out there?

III

They saw vastly different things in each other:
the fisher folk eyed objects of trade,
markets for their smoked fish, kente cloth,
the slavers objects of labor. No way
would their interests coincide.

Did they hear cries from below,
those slavers on top taking sex
from their charges? What did they smell
as they took their meals?

In the stonewalled gloom, I listen
for manacled feet and cries of the bound,
hear only the retreating the returning waves,
and the call of gulls.

The Africa Thing

What is Africa to us?

Let's shuffle

Paint that horn
on backwards—
Knock me some skin   Blow! O

They say home
is a place
in the mind
where you
can rest
when you're tired
not where
your great great
great grandfather
had his farm

Africa?

Africa   beble be
is that old man   ba
in the pickin field   bo
making that strange high sound   bibob
and all the people following   blaaba
Africa is a sound   ba ba

Africa   buddi di oooooo
is the touch   rock a diooooo
of that old woman
your mother could not stand   do oo do o
but did respect
who caught you as you fell

and held you
and rocked you

Fat black bucks in a wine barrel			boom
boom
what is Africa to us				bam
fee thou thoo thum				boom
I smell the sweat of English scum			boom boom

—Mamma, Mamma, but he does
It's *not* just his breath
He stink
Hushsssh, chile
Somebody'll hear you
Say *smell.*

Africa
is the look
of Tweebie Mae
snapping her
head around
before she took off
	Caint ketch me
in the soft dark
You caught her

Africa
is all them roots
and conjures
and spells
wails and chants
(say blues and hollers)
and all them stories
about Stackalee
and John Henry
and Bo Diddley
and the camp meetings
where the wrestling

and head and head
the foot races
the jumping
the throwing

We brought all that down

to dance at birth
when you're sick
take a wife
lose your luck
when you die

and singing in the woods
     in the fields
   when you walk
and singing on the levies
     on the chain gang
     in the jail
singing and dancing when you pray
and dancing by the light of the moon
until you drop.

Africa is the singing
of these lines
of me
of you
of love
singing.

Blues Fugue

The Mr. and Mrs.

Long retired, fearing the uselessness
of old age; not trained to counsel or to teach
he scavenges with a shopping cart.

His route loops around wherever
night people toss their empties. He works
the jagged edges: gutters, park trash cans, the tracks.

Before daybreak I hear hard plastic wheels
send shock waves through stone. By sun up
he returns, as I am opening the gate for a friend.

Shirt stuffed in overalls, cigar stub clamped
in left molars, his high-pitched voice odd
out of his heavy frame, he complains about his feet

I tell him not to worry. I know he is one
link in the industrial chain, and his feet
do get him there and back.

His scavenger wife will not scavenge with him
though they may leave at the same time
they never go together. He takes his direction

she hers. He takes a cart, she a big plastic bag
and a stick for dogs. Her voice sings like his
rising from deeper in the throat. She

throws herself into movement, rocking
ever forward. The sort of woman who
won't stand still for a hug.

Pin clean herself, she laments
too few share her passion. She sweeps
the sidewalk, gutter, around the corner even.

She drives and drags him as she drives
herself. Only he is too stubborn
to be dragged too fast or too far.

She pouts. She talks about him
like you would a dog. "He's lazy.
Got no ambition. Never had none."

A faithful churchgoer, she rags him
to chauffeur her when she can (she has
blown her license running red lights).

For all her bad mouthing, they stay together.
Hooked like crabs, they hang on, not
so much to each other but to marriage.

That is what they know. My single state
is both temptation and threat to them.
Neither would survive it a week, nor each other.

Coda

Although he did die without her
she remains ever more active
covering his route as well as her own.

"God has taken him," she says
"He wanted him more than me."

Always with the strength of two
she bangs around illegally in her
fifteen-year-old Plymouth

Now that he is dead she speaks
only his praise. How he thought
of her, planned for her in his last days

I am chastened.
For who would dare question
the mystery of couples, the

miracle of how and why
they stay connected?

Maudelle

Work all day
Beat from that hag on your neck
Come home to make dinner
for the kids
He there reading sports
Watching television with his beer
on his beer belly
You done start the night mad.

You wonder sometimes
that newspapers don't tell him
or TV,
That times have changed
Woman can't have no hag on her neck
And man on her back

Maybe one of those
TV programs tell him
How come his bed
Feel like ice.

When I go to sleep under a man
Got to be one I can trust
Not some
      run-in
      slup
      bam
I'm gone,
And I awake watching
Worrying about next week's groceries

But when I know
He's going to be around
Through the tight times
When my opening up won't mean I'm bound
To eat dust and drink lonely wine
I can sleep three deep
And dream me some dreams.

She giving, what for; he giving, what for?

It must have been a badly arranged
marriage. They both brought their

complaints with them on to the train
she in his face, he in hers.

He no bigger than she; she younger
stronger. I did not need

to know Chinese to see they wore
wrong yokes. Their constant bickering

had cut ruts in their voices.

He Died in His Hurry

Big Yoruba man, she smaller
Ibo woman. He push, she push;
They push, he push harder. Heart snaps.
He die. All for the kids.

What kid want to be kid
In that family? Rush, rush
Everywhere. Brush your teeth,
Brush your hair, brush your hair.
Rub on skin cream, work it in.
Tie your shoes.

Good neighbors! Give you shirt
Off their backs. House, yard?
Clean, fresh paint, no weeds.

Not a smudge on the picture window.

A Blues

back on the rack

lost my track

no wonder my blues so bad

woman done left me

boss on my tail

got no money to make my bail

lost my track

back on the rack

no wonder my blues so bad

"A" Train Uptown

to Sharon Olds

I'd love to sleep
But I'll miss my stop
Or get rolled

I need the sleep

The class and the job
Sometimes
Feel like cutting one loose
Cut the job
Don't eat now
Cut the class
Don't eat later

Pay your money
Don't get much

What's that across from me,
Like she giving me the eyescan
Like she don't want to stare
Just get a good peep

I can dig it

What you think you see
You with your joke pearls
Wrapped up in dead cats

Think you cool
Lame as you are
White fantasy bubble
Furred and too fat
Curves that used to bring you men
Settling into double chin

I'm beat
But Eartha Mae's waiting
Meat and a beer
And Fred's there

Gotta get him a job
Been up here too long
Little brother be damned

Think she's seen enough
Gripping her bag tighter
Wonder what she'd do
If I said, "Boo!"

From Our Full-Service Station

She was driving though she seemed driven,
the child standing, arms around her neck.
Did the child know she had tried it before?

I didn't.

She only wanted gas, nothing more
when so much more was offered.

She was a brilliant woman,
maybe that is why.

A lover to her husband told me later,
*He was a cold man, he would
Manipulate you to death.*

Maybe that is why she left the child
at her mother's, and put the shotgun
in her mouth.

If a tree falls in the forest...

Who would hear

her scream

as he forces himself

past her final boundary,

deep in the forest,

end of the corn row,

edge of the rice paddy,

off the trail,

in the maid's closet,

back of his buddy's pick-up;

and with noise of countless

generations trying

to muffle her,

in their bed?

The Moving Target Should Not Slow

Blood was splattered
over chairs, sofa; on walls; in the fish
tank, so she had fought. She did not
go gentle, but he was stronger, and
had the benefit of partial surprise.

She knew he might beat her, if she put
herself in his way. He had beaten his
female lawyer, who had made the mistake
of mixing pleasure in her business with
a psychotic client. Beat her, yes, but
kill her, that she never dreamed.

*In California state prisons, no matter
what your sentence, you have to be good
to get out. Some prisoners are simply
never good enough.*

They had been lovers once.

He had awakened the woman in her,
she said, long dormant through
her struggle in the men's world.
She was a successful business woman
but it had cost the part of her
that was tender, and could respond
to love. He had brought alive a part
she had thought dead.

Why did she let him in that night?
She had a restraining order, he was not
to go near her. She would be a fool,
with what she knew, to let him in.

Out of The Horn, a Cry

Big and Africa, slight and Africa.

They are black from Africa, The Horn:
Eritrea, Somaliland, Ethiopia,
thin delicate features, soot black,
burning intense eyes.

Their clothes are not in fashion.

Our country has been receiving refugees
from Menghistu.

She is speaking softly, intently,
He answers with grunts, looking across
the street, up the tracks, at the sky,
everywhere but at her.

She attends to him fully, her eyes focused;
softly, lips parted, sound flows up
from her center, arms making circles.

Is his boredom an act? Is he supposed
to ignore her in public? Where is she pulling/
pushing him to? Why is he not going?

Why I Sing the Blues

You think the blues are bad,

that they bring on sadness.

How could you be so wrong?

You tell me not to sing

the blues, I'll say you mad

and don't know blues.

I sing the blues so they

won't stay around today.

I sing the blues to drive

the blues away.

Praise, Praise Music

Music reaching a sky free of sky-gods
Music of the earth
    From the earth
    Metals from the mines
    Reeds from the fields
    From the woods roll the drums
Praise the folk, praise Four Blind Boys

Praise Grover Washington, Jr., Praise Bach,
    Kent Nagano, Jon Jang, Anthony Davis,
    Buffy St. Marie, Ali Akbar Khan
    Quila Pajun, Inti-Illimani

A.K. Black who played a sky-god
in Benjamin Britten's *Noah*…
who rapped an "Introduction to Destruction"
that blew us all away. Praise eco-rap!

Laurie Anderson, John Cage, Frank Zappa

Rosalyn Tureck is Ms. Bach, but I heard her
with my own ears stomp out a boogie woogie.
Praise Bach, praise Boogie-Woogie.

Hey baba lee bop! Hey baba lee bop!
Praise the folk, praise Kitka,
Praise Howling Wolf and Bartok and Duke

    Nancy Wilson
    Went to town
    Riding on a pony
    Stuck a feather in her hair
    And Hey, now!

This body, this tube out of which
miraculous sounds pour; O miracle
this body

    Clap your hands
    Beat your thighs
    Slap your chest
    Stomp you feet

Listen to the sounds, listen to the music, yes
Oh clap your hands, whenever you want to
Clap your hands whenever you want to

    Praise music
    Praise music
    Praise

Bach Had His Blues

J. S. Bach would have loved the blues,

With all those children he fathered,

he would know the feeling.

Blues take you down then lift

you up. Bach does that.

Bach too likes to worry a line,

like spinning on a dime.

Dig those fugues and variations.

My boy JS could stand with Louie

and Duke, and not take low,

the sho nuff bluesman that he was.

Four Tops Live at The Roostertail

to Al Young

Duke and the back-up band wailed
"Ask the Lonely." A Sister called,
"Can I help you out?" Duke answered,
"I wish to *god* you could."

Mellow together, music and crowd, that night
you'd think a *Motown* night at The Roostertail:
Marvin Gaye, Isley Brothers, the Supremes,
all dropped by to give Duke and The Four Tops
a boost. Watts not on their minds at all.

Aretha was on one of her record-breaking,
body-bending tours. On the road she caught
Nina singing "Go limp" to too drunk white folk who
clapped, then choked on, "Mississippi, Goddamn!"
Water hoses and police dogs on Nina's mind.

Was their Titanic shaking toward fire and ice?
Was it Nero night at The Roostertail,
where they drank their drinks, danced their dance,
sang their song and didn't want to go home?

Ask the lonely, love *don't* come easy, will
you tell me please, *please, please, what's going on?*

Milk Run

Tokyo burning at nine o'clock.
We're heading north to Hokkaido.
Been on fire some time now,

wood and paper, uneven smoke piles,
snow on Fuji, imperfect sunrise.
Trapped like rats under collapsing frames.

Tell it to *Admiral* Tojo.

Squadron Double O peeling off,
headed west. Japan Sea.
"Let's play tag." That's my wingman,

the fool. *"Nothing else to do."* He
is right, of course. These missions
are a bore. How can I tell my boy

I knocked down zeroes when we
haven't seen one in months?
"Let's window shop. Down to 2, 1.5.

Waggle our wings. Why, I'll be Christ,
if they're not waving back."
Scuttlebutt has it, enemy suing

for peace. Seven more of these
milk runs and I can go home
sweet home. Hear we're gonna

drop a big one down south, maybe
something monster. Lots of hush, hush
about it. Enola Gay's off limits

past two weeks. Bundles of Dear Johns
every mail call. Lots of crews all shook up.
Not my worry, I don't think. I do

wish she'd learn to handle money better.
O to see her face.

"Rendezvous for base return."
Gotta ditch the ord. No targets.
Can't take it back to Mama.

Our *"little war in the Pacific"* may soon
be over, none too soon for me.

Boys that boasted, *"We'll be home
for Christmas,"* forgot to say
which one.

Shore Patrol

> "You can arrest the President, it's wartime."
> *Who, me?*

I could arrest the President?
What did our CPO mean? Arrest
our Commander-in-Chief? What could
our President do that I would want
to jail him?

Ice-laden, hawk-driven snow off Lake Michigan.
If this was once Indian land, couldn't we give it back?
All of twenty, Shore Patrol arm band, night
stick in my belt, I walked the shore, after
being dumped at Waukegan's city square
with my fellows.

Had to walk this out, this surge of scary
power. The President—forget fancy, what
was I to do about my classmates and others
from the Base who staggered or fell?
Would I help them up or beat them down?

I had the power. Through me coursed the might
of the world's top fighting machine. I could
feel pumped up muscles, blood running despite
the biting cold. I swung my arms, backed by
the Navy, Army, Air Force, the Marines.

In my euphoria I slipped on a piece of snow
covered ice and plunged into a bush.
On my feet after struggle, I brushed myself,
smoothed out my dress blues, looked around
to see who might have seen.

No one. I was safe.
Attention! Forward, march!

The Obscenities

hate,
rape,
bomb,
kill

all four
letter words

stop and
stop and
stop, too
as is
love

I need exponential language
words raised to the nth power
to explain how I feel
about what's coming down;
how else can I express dismay squared
or the cube of sorrow?

Street Scenes 1993

Used to be they
thought we were crazy
Not so hard on us then
Now they say we criminal
Watch out

Checked his blue
flak jacket before
I hung it on the railing
by the post office
Plastic razor, some
cookie crumbs
a plastic dab of mustard
from a fast food joint

Given: the rich get theirs
Given: rest of us scuffle
over what's left

A reporter
came by here
asked me
what was my
vantage point
I said I had
no vantage point

People study us
a lot

Never ask
why we are
poor
We'd ask them
to look in the mirror

Saw that
crippled poet
the other day
She writes poems
about us
Nice to have
someone write poems
about us

Every night
the dark comes
and I'm scared

They spent
more money
trying to find
her people
after she died
than when
she was
hungry

Talk about
the shelters
like they some
heaven
They ever
sleep in one?

Watching the Flea Circus She Thought

Watching the fleas

the little girl thought,

why not find the right pitch

for the fleas, the best tone,

the right rhythm?

Make them dance; free up

the dogs and cats;

keep them dancing,

dance themselves silly,

then die happy.

Color Picture of a Beaten Boxer

He sits,
sweat glistening on gloves
signals a hard worked day.

Bronzed shoulders,
bright like his clenched hands,
hunch too far forward.

Golden Gloves.

He sits,
trying to picture what went wrong
while he was still on his feet,
how he could neither roll with the right cross
nor step inside the left hook.

Slate eyes say
he will not challenge
for the Gold.

The Square Ring

You get them in trouble,
A man told Sugar Ray.
It's my business
to get them in trouble,
Sugar Ray told the man.

Hot lights, crowd chanting his name,
adrenalin shoots through his fear.
At the bang of the bell he is alone.
Hands between him, shame and destruction.
Pain he must master, fear he must conceal.

His opponent seeks to thunder
leather on his skull, plunder
him of his senses. Jab, jab, feint,
move, jab, cross, move, move, move.
He can't confuse the fake for the blow.

He must draw his opponent in,
lure him, trap him, upset
his timing, break him, make him weep.

Jab, jab, move, feint, cross, jab, move, move.
He knows the ring is not a safe place
for children or the unafraid.

Under the glare of lights, eyes of the crowd,
he is more exposed than the corner back,
goalie, pitcher, point man, blues man,
monologist; he is toreador
with a thinking foe.

As the rounds add, the ring subtracts.
Time expands.
What is that opening he sees? It may
not come again. Entree or snare?
Is this the moment for the left hook?

What are you scheming, trickster man?
One swing away from heaven or from hell.

Stolen Peace at Windover

for John Turner

So peaceful in here, she said.
Yes, he sighed.
They looked down over red roofs.
Breeze pressed against her face
through a crack in the window.
They looked at the black pine
and clouds that scraped the bay.

Their minds turned to their worlds outside.
Her hand in his grew limp,
"I shan't come again."
It has been peaceful here, he said.

Rationalization For Not Writing More

Three o'clock.
This time of morning
I should be shifting dreams.

Maybe if the desk were nearer,
I would write more.
That is the Reason I give myself:
the typewriter, the desk, the table.

Typewriter lugged, desk
and table dragged from the place
they have earned in my study,
to be close to my bed

Voila! Presto! Eureka!

All I need now is pop up
when an idea surfaces,
ease over to the machine
and bang away.

Yet a nagging doubt persists.

There's something too easy
about this merely mechanical solution.

My doubt says shift the furniture
of the head around, throw
the chairs and tables of the brain
into place.

The Galileans

Two common criminals
And a political prisoner,
That's how they think it was.

Well, I was up there
because they said I stole something.
Nothing political about that.

Cat was not much whiter than I was.
Came on talking all that off the wall stuff,
like, the meek shall inherit the earth.
Then he'd contradict himself,

the poor shall always be with you.
Well, I didn't take no always being poor.
I had worked hard, *hard,*
in the fields, the mines, on the waterfront;

No matter how much or how hard I worked,
I never got out from under.
I make it, taxes get it.
tried share cropping, landlord take it.
Had kids to feed; kept my nose clean
till then.

Have you seen Appian Way?
See any rich men on them crosses?
They're all poor like me, and black or brown,
or crazies like him they call political.

Cat tried to 'save' me for his God.
Hell, I wanted to be cut down.
Now, is that political or what?

I would have followed the cat,
I mean, if he really wanted to stone get down
and tear the mother up, but he didn't.
He was only into just some jive time reforms.
Judas had the right idea.
Like it wasn't a color, it's a system.

I'm not a snitch or nothing,
I wouldn't have fingered the cat;
but he was talking trash, *trash,*
and I for damn sure couldn't go where he led.

The Saga of Francis O. Penniman

> There is a forest burning and we need
> everyone who can fetch a pail.
>   – Paule Marshall, *Daughters*

Out of the group of us that began publishing
then, we all agreed that Francis O.
Penniman had the most talent and that he would
be the one to soar.

After some years his output was still meager,
the score: a few novels, all near misses,
dull plays, featureless films (he had tried to take
Hollywood by storm and found Hollywood wasn't
buying). "They aren't ready for me," he boasted.
"You just wait." We waited. For all his bluster,
he produced nothing meaty enough to chew on
or funny enough to laugh at cleanly.

Things came too easy too early for Francis
O. Penniman. He read stories about himself
and preened himself on them. He believed
the Oracles that told him success
was his for the picking. He read the stories
but did not read the oracle right.
When the two lines were laid out, he
chose the one that told him success
could be his for the picking.

So he picked, and misused his talent,
wasted his money on himself, women and wine,
lied to his friends, used and deserted them.
Became a caricature of Big Man: The Writer.

He left a trail not so much of broken
as disgusted hearts. What was wrong
with the brother? We who knew him
early on lamented, "When will that cat
ever shape up?"

There were arguments: He will, he won't.
He'll never be in love with no body but Francis.
I, too, said that he might never shape up, but
then, coward that I am, I hedged. People change,
I said, people change. He might.
He's still young, someone conceded, maybe
his emotional intelligence will improve.
That suggestion drew a guffaw from the skeptics.

O. Penniman was another poor bright Southerner
snapped up by an Ivy League school,
in the same generation as Clarence Thomas.
The Scholarship Boy label was no less excruciating
for him at Yale than for George Orwell at Eton.
Some of his writing showed he had not strayed
too far from the folk.

Few years ago, I looked out from pruning
roses and saw Francis O. Penniman
jogging past my front yard to the college gym.
Huffing and puffing, I mean he was
laying down some rubber

"Way to go, Man!" I shouted. He gave
me a modified Black Panther salute and laughed,
"Gotta off this flab,"
pointing to the inner tube
round his belly.

Even in his heyday of parties and women,
I always felt there was something about him
that ran scared, that a lot of his bragging was
for show.

On one of my monthly trips
to the library basement stacks,
there he was, almost hidden
by books piled head high.

"Ph.D?" I asked.

"Yeah, man, gotta get that union card."
He tossed in, off-handedly,
 "And I'm working on
some personal stuff."

I wasn't too surprised then, when
Dr. Penniman wrote a well received childhood
memoir, and has pushed his scholarly weight
into the fight for the beleaguered
black male.

He has taken on the anti-rap
critics in articles that place rap within
oral traditions reaching back to African Griots,
even to the blind Greek Homer.

My jury, of course, is still out, it is
too soon to tell (two robins do not a summer
make), but it is leaning towards acquittal.

I expect the brother to fetch his pail.

Tell My Heart

You Asked for Rain

You asked for rain, I brought thunder.
You asked about tomorrow and I shied away
from predictions. I could handle today,
but who would follow the unknown?

Nestmaker, your search was for land
and a protected space.
I, herder, put my faith in cattle and dreams.

Like rails we were, switched by fate
and that turn in our lives, into a crossing.
Crossing we joined and travelled a short way together,
but like rails, again we sprung apart.

I needed the woman in you then, to cement
the man in me. What you needed was

not protection, really. You knew at base
your bulwark was yourself. You needed,
as you said, a partner to join you in the dance.

But I, no mean dancer, could not hack it.
You were too many for me, too many
and too swift, your turkey in the straw
too much for my slow drag.

Tell My Heart

Tell my heart
that promises are off,
vows are retracted,
leased love let loose,
    tell it.

    Tell my heart
it has no bond,
is no longer allied;
    tell it
to stop its longing,
its yearning to hold,
be held, enfold.

    Tell it
never again to slip earth's bounds
never again to soar.

    You tell my heart,
        You,
    for I cannot.

I Hoped You Would Stay

I wanted you to come and you did.
You came and you stayed,
then you left.

I hoped you would come and you came.
You came, you stayed and stayed,
then you went away.

I prayed you would come but you didn't.
I begged you to come but you wouldn't.

I look to see the sway in your walk,
or your skip. After all, it is spring,
when sap rises, and geese return.

You took our dream when you left,
When you left you took my breath.

I see them now these words of love
implanted under the hill, that opened
the leaf, the bud, the flower,
the forever never words no doubt can faze.

You go but you can never leave.
Spirit is in the rock, the tree,
rush of the wind, the sea.

I wanted you to come, you came,
you did, and stayed, in me.

After Reading Fred Johnston's "Folk Song"

You sing this truth of Jane
and Joe, Kofi and Ama Ata,
Lai Wah and Ko. I hear you
as the tune starts low
then rises and spreads.

It is the worry of the soul,
how we all love, want to love,
be loved. You know that time,
space, age place no barrier
to sorrow. Heartbreak is
the coin we spend.

"The Heart Has Its Reasons"

Absence makes the heart grow
empty.

> Mwindo, Congolese epic hero,
> stayed away hunting
> in the deep forest for many years,
> returned to find two healthy
> girls and a boy.
>
> "Wife, what is this?" he stormed.
> With great calm she answered,
> "Had to have them while I could."

Distance creates vacuum in the heart.
Distance makes a special kind of absence,
It makes the heart grow abstract.

> We who know the Tale of the Ancient
> Mariner know he sailed the seas for years,
> rode out many's the storm.
>
> The family he saw
> through the window of his house
> that night when he got back
> was his, not his,
> but the man's who was settled with them.
>
> He had been absent
> too long. He knew it,
> so he left.

Homer tells us Odysseus,
home from the wars
and his wandering,
found his Penelope
weaving and chaste.

Weaving, yes, but chaste?
Blind Homer tells us this.

Absence holds no brief for chastity.

Nature is one penalty men bear
who go off to war, go on
the road to sell.

Absence wearies the heart,
leaves the arms with nothing to hold.
Nature abhors a vacuum,
they say.

Foolish, foolish men.

Absence makes the heart grow
empty.

...Keeps the Doctor...

Writing John Cage's
    Poem a day

Josephine Miles
    Could do it

She had us write
    Minute poems

I wrote mine about
    Love lost
And regained

I was not
    Into sadness
    Then

The Harvest

How remote they are as they lie there
Gathering the colors of love.
He remembers shoots bursting to sunlight,

The tenderest of greens,
A quiet sea, amethyst,
Radiant as the idea of a star.

She remembers rasping sand
Sugar-fine and dry
The puncture of thistles,

Ay!

He remembers love the colors of dreams
And she the colors of night.

The Rescue

to e.c.

The cookies
Came at the exact time
I needed them

I was in shock from a bad rap
Had been low-rated, called a name

by Anonymous

Your chocolate chips, a
delicious public presentation
set my gyro back on course

Some would let this teacher starve,
you would not; nor would you chunk
a rock then hide your hand

Five Green Years

Even after you returned my bond

and said, *I'll stay*, we

still didn't know how long.

As long as love lasts. Not a stable

basis for a marriage. For

an affair. Yes. Perfect for that.

Peculiar madness, love. But

we've survived five green years

and thrived. Economy in the black,

blue days at a minimum.

We are new people. We love

with passion. Gold glow in warm dark.

The Anniversary

They say one has to be a little mad
To marry.
There must have been times
you wanted to call it quits
but you didn't,
times you wondered why.

Till death do us part:
Powerful words, uttered only
by the young or foolish.
They say one has to be
A little mad to marry.

Sometimes it is good
to simply live long enough,
balancing 'store with loss' and loss with gain.

To stay married you go beyond love.
You learn to change
and accept change.

It is always a modest joy
we end up with.

The Heart

After the mind goes, the heart stays,
tracking treasures no thought can conjure.
The beat of feet, light to my door
will bring songs soon. I can hear them.

Cornucopia heart, empty out
high notes, falsetto or true,
so we can snatch love sounds
now. Do. While there is still time
within this hour to shout.

Riding the Range of Thought

to J. Waller, MD

Will have to smash all thoughts before I can sleep.
One near coherent one will make my mind try
endlessly to tighten its meander.

Come back here. Can't be shootin no chitlins
at no moon, leaping over no razor wire chasms,
climbing no squash yellow sky.

Let's bargain. Wait. If you permit me to grab
a few winks tonight, yes, just a few, I'll play scrabble
with you tomorrow, or solitaire. Name your game.

Smash *you* to smithereens? No, no nothing
like that. Here, take this chocolate-coated
lollipop. Sweet, sweet thought, just come
a little closer, just a little closer.

Dreamscape

It was your letter
that pushed me on
that warm up winter.

The years' retreats were many, advances few.
Blowing sand clogged my engine
I ran with apples falling,
persimmons crying.

I watched too many best friends die.

Udders of white cows
hung heavy for the millions.

You said,
field is fallow, not dead
furrow it again,
come spring.

NOTES

"Keep Sending Love Out," appeared in *Land Between: New and Selected Poems.*

"Full of Flying Things" was written after reading Tz'u poems of the Sung Dynasty translated by Julie Landau, *Beyond Spring,* Columbia University Press, 1994.

In "Good Friday on Bear Valley Trail, 1978," "my Shadow" refers to Ibo cosmology, in which there is a shadow world identical to our own.

In "Four Tops Live at The Roostertail," The Roostertail is a Detroit nightspot, popular during the Motown era.

In "Women at the Fence, at the Well," "crone" refers to the fact that contemporary women have established crones and witches as women of wisdom.

In "Shorty the Iceman," Miss Bronson the fifth grade teacher was working as a maid. It was not unusual for colored teachers to spend their summers Up North, working "in service" to supplement their meager pay. Finding his teacher working so close to home was a surprise for the young boy.

These poems were previously published in other collections before appearing in *Ticket to Exile*: "My Trip," "Night Trip Downtown" appeared in *Apocalypse is My Garden.* "My Dog When I Was Seven," "While I Thought God, My Mother Saw," and "My Mother Washed Other People's Clothes," appeared in *Neighborhood and Other Poems.* "Night on the Town" and "Graduation" appeared in *Land Between.*

"Sunday Visit to a Carolina Chain Gang": After Emancipation, former slaves were arrested on a myriad of petty charges and held on impossibly high bail until some white farmer or plant owner paid their fines and bound them into peonage and perpetual debt.

"Planes of View" is a Hurricane Katrina poem written September 17, 2005. Algiers is a District of New Orleans that was only slightly affected by flooding.

ADAM DAVID MILLER was born in 1922, in Dorchester County, South Carolina. He has served the arts community in the San Francisco Bay Area for four decades as a teacher, writer, editor, publisher, radio and television programmer and producer. An award winning poet and author, he edited *Dices or Black Bones: Black Voices of the Seventies*, recipient of the California Teachers Association Award for best anthology. His own collection, *Forever Afternoon*, won the first Naomi Long Madgett Poetry Award in 1994. His poem, "African Woman Casts Her Shadow," won First Prize in the Artists Embassy International Dancing Poetry Contest. *Ticket to Exile*, a memoir, was a finalist for the Northern California Book Award in Creative Nonfiction, 2008, and was one of three finalists in Nonfiction for the William Saroyan International Prize for Writing, 2008. He was awarded the Berkeley Poetry Festival lifetime achievement award in 2011, for which the City of Berkeley proclaimed a day in his honor. Adam David Miller taught in California schools and colleges, ending his formal career at the University of California, Berkeley. With his Aldridge Players West, a black-run theater group, he acted, directed, and, during the Civil Rights Era, traveled with his company to black-run colleges. He sought out new playwrights, some African and Caribbean. As a National Endowment for the Humanities Fellow 1973-74, he traveled widely in west Africa, returning to Africa twice. He also traveled in Europe, the Caribbean, and Mexico. Frequently featured as a poet and workshop leader at reading venues, schools, and colleges throughout the nation and abroad, he makes his home in Berkeley, California.

The Sky is a Page: New & Selected Poems was printed on acid free paper. The typeface is Adobe Caslon Pro. The title page and section title pages feature ink wash illustrations by Jinny Pearce.